W9-BAH-656

WONDERWISE™
Cars

Published by Smart Apple Media,
an imprint of Black Rabbit Books
P.O. Box 3263, Mankato, Minnesota 56002
www.blackrabbitbooks.com

Published by arrangement with
The Salariya Book Company Ltd

Cataloging-in-Publication Data is available
from the Library of Congress

Printed in the United States
At Corporate Graphics,
North Mankato, Minnesota

9 8 7 6 5 4 3 2 1

ISBN: 978-1-62588-359-9

Illustrators: Mark Bergin
Nick Hewetson
Gerald Wood
David Antram
Tony Townsend

WONDERWISE™

Cars

DAVID MILLER

A+
Smart Apple Media

CONTENTS

INTRODUCTION

The 21st century is the age of the car. We travel by car so often that it is hard to imagine how we would get around without one. But did you know that the first cars were built more than a hundred years ago? People stopped and stared at these strange "horseless carriages" smoking and sputtering in the streets. Compared to the cars today, even cars from the 1960s and 1970s look like they belong in a museum. Cars of the future may be self-driving, safer, and even able to run without fossil fuels.

ON THE ROAD

Today's streets are jammed with cars. Whether they are going to school, work, the store, or even on vacation, millions of people choose to drive. Cars can carry not only people, but all their baggage too.

▼ Police cars have sirens, radios, and specially adapted engines.

▲ City streets are crowded with traffic, especially during weekday mornings and evenings. This is called the rush hour.

In the city, traveling by public transport—bus, subway, or train—is often quicker than driving.

Most cars are family cars. But there are also many special-purpose cars, like taxis, and police cars. Sports cars are built for speed, while off-road vehicles are made for rugged cross-country driving.

▼ Trucks are large, powerful vehicles that transport cargo from place to place.

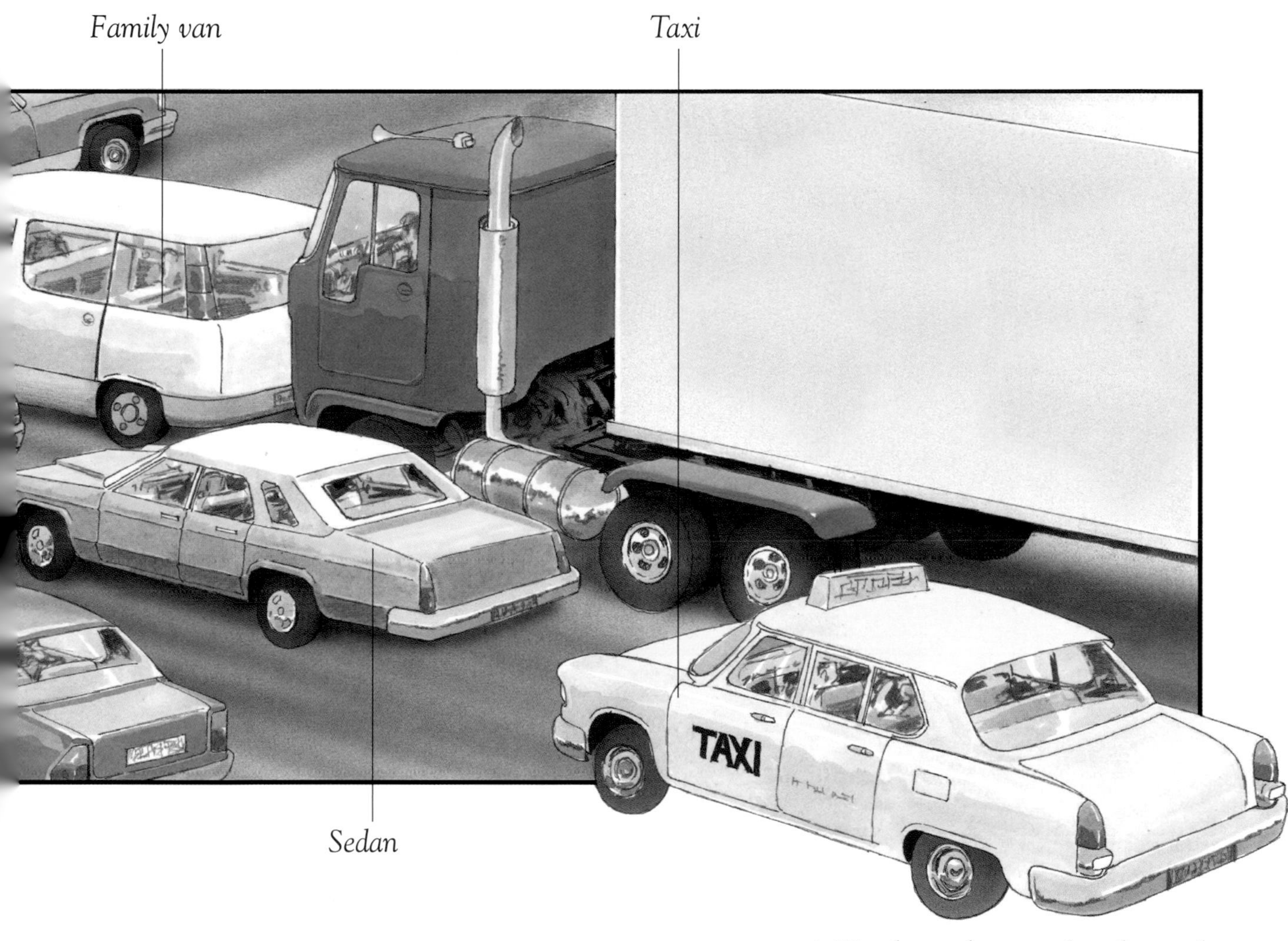

▶ Away from home, people often get around by using taxis or even hiring a car.

▲ Trucks and vans often have their sides painted. Sometimes this is just for decoration, but often it is to advertise a company or product.

THE FIRST CARS

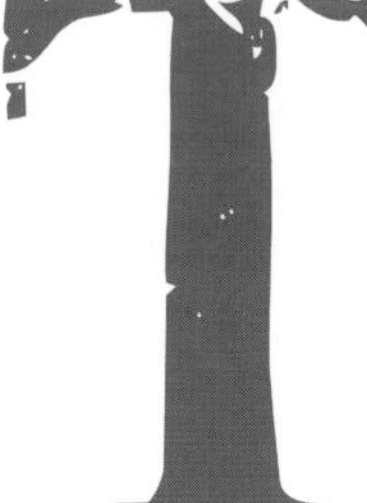

The first cars were slow, rickety, smoky, and incredibly noisy. They were known as "horseless carriages" because they looked like traditional carriages but were driven by an engine instead of a horse.

▲ *British electric car* l'Elephant, *one of six electric entries in the 1898 Auto Club de France, Paris—Amsterdam race.*

▲ The Frenchman Nicolas-Joseph Cugnot built a three-wheeled steam-powered tractor in 1769. This clumsy vehicle went almost 3 miles per hour (5 kph), stopping every 15 minutes.

▶ Gasoline-powered engines were developed in the late 1880s. One of the first gasoline-driven cars was this tricycle made by Karl Benz in 1885 in Germany.

◀ Early cars looked like the horse-drawn carriages they were replacing. Both the 1895 Panhard et Levassor and 1894 Peugeot went faster with their hoods down. This showed the importance of streamlining vehicles to reduce wind-resistance.

Steering column

The horn was squeezed by hand.

The steering wheel was very hard to turn. All sorts of controls were mounted on the steering column.

To get it started, the engine had to be cranked up by hand. Electric starters were not common until the 1930s.

The hand brake was released slowly, while the driver put the car in gear and gently took his or her foot off the clutch pedal.

Hand brake

▲ The De Dion Bouton Model Q was a French "runabout" of 1903. It had a speedy little engine. Early motorists wore special clothes to protect them from smoke, dust, and weather. Cars had no roof or windshield, so drivers often wore goggles.

The lights were brass lamps that burned oil or gasoline. They made driving at night a real adventure.

THE CAR TAKES OVER

▲ *The White Steamer of 1903 had its engine at the front and a boiler coiled under the driver's seat.*

Early cars were made by hand. They were beautiful but expensive. In the early 1900s, the rich drove luxury cars like the famous Rolls-Royce. In 1908 Henry Ford introduced the first cheap car, the Model T Ford. It was mass-produced on a factory assembly line. For the first time ordinary people could afford a car.

▲ *The "Spirit of Ecstasy" ornament was added to the Rolls-Royce hood in 1909.*

Folding top

Hood

Wooden spokes

A chauffeur is a professional driver who looks after a car and drives people around.

▲ The Rolls-Royce 40/50 was nicknamed the "Silver Ghost" because its engine was so quiet.

The Ford Motor Company was founded in Detroit, Michigan, in 1903. It is still one of the world's biggest carmakers.

Henry Ford told his customers they could have a Model T Ford in "any color you like as long as it's black."

All the parts of a Model T Ford were made separately. Workers on an assembly line bolted them together.

▲ In 1908, when the Model T Ford was launched, fewer than 200,000 Americans owned a car. Nineteen years later, more than 15 million had been sold in the U.S. alone.

▲ "Tin Lizzy" was the name given to the Model T. It looked rickety compared to handmade cars, but it proved to be strong and reliable.

A DREAM MACHINE

The Bugatti Royale Type 41 was a spectacular luxury car. It was more stylish than a Rolls-Royce—and three times more expensive. Only six were ever made, and only three sold. The engine alone was as big as many modern cars.

The huge engine had eight cylinders and used 3.35 gallons (12.7 L) of fuel. It weighed 770 pounds (349 kg)—the same as five grown men.

▶ *Different Bugatti models*

This elegant car was extremely long at 22 feet (6.7 m). But it could turn corners smoothly.

Mudflap

Pneumatic tires

By the 1920s, most cars were mass-produced. But every part of the Bugatti Royale was made by hand. The customer discussed all the detail with the designer, Ettore Bugatti. The car was then built to suit the customer's taste and style. No two cars were the same.

▼ *The famous Bugatti ornament, an elephant, sat above the radiator. It combined the name of the Italian designer and the French company he set up.*

The Bugatti Royale is worth even more money now. In 1987, a secondhand Royale sold for $9.5 million.

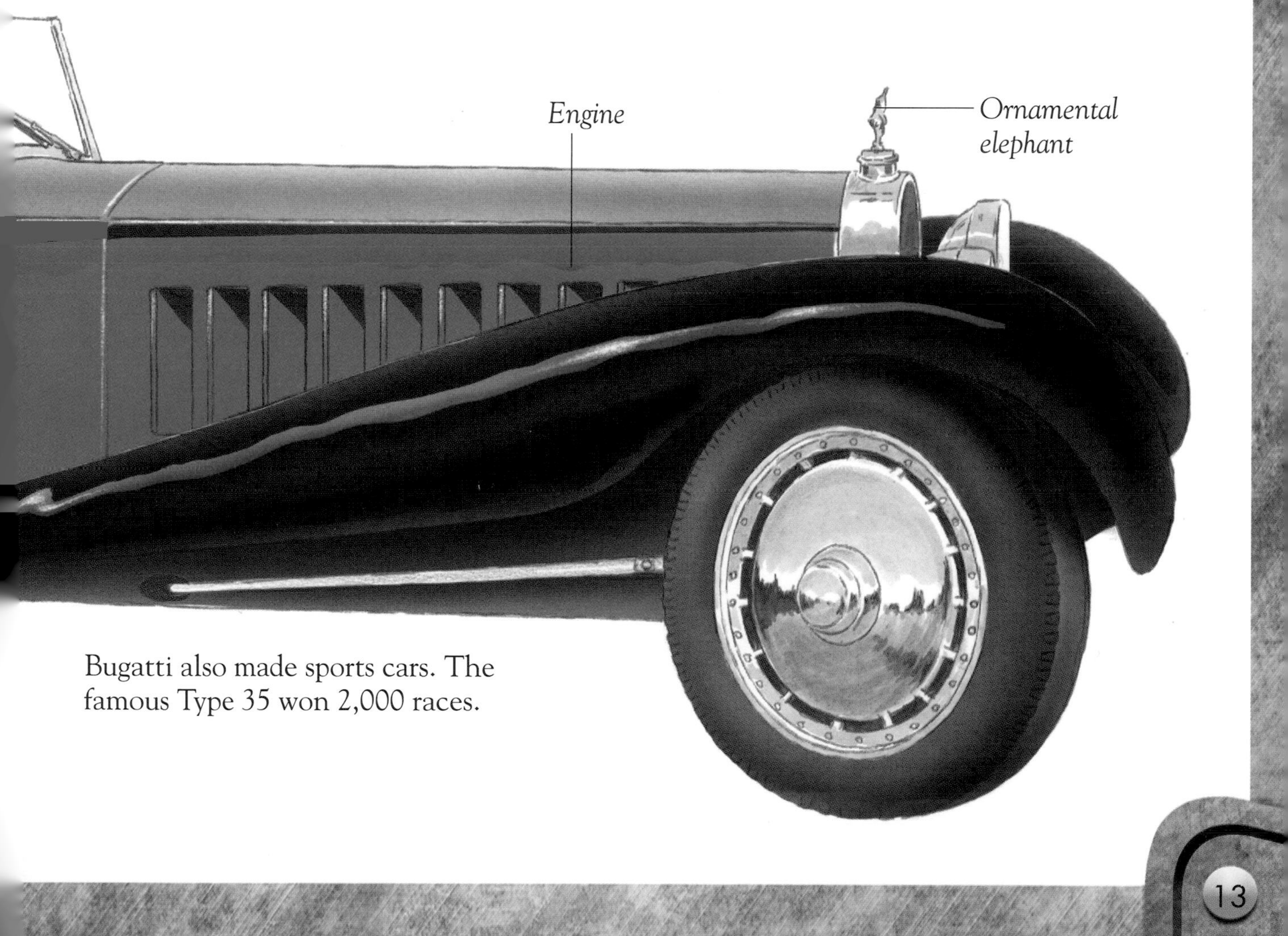

Bugatti also made sports cars. The famous Type 35 won 2,000 races.

THE FORTIES

World War Two (1939–1945) was the first truly motorized war. In World War One (1914–1918) cars had been used to some extent. But motor transport was not an essential part of the struggle. German military planners were the first to realize how motorized transport could change warfare.

Canvas top

Masked headlamps *Spare wheel*

▲ *During the war the Volkswagen "people's car" was converted into the military* Kübelwagen *by designer, Dr Ferdinand Porsche.*

▲The Volkswagen's pre-war body was replaced by an easily produced slab-sided box. The weight of the rear engine over the driving wheels gave good grip on loose surfaces and General Rommel used it in the desert war (1941–1943).

◀ In 1940, the U.S. army four-wheel-drive Jeep (for GP or General Purpose) became world famous. Its four-wheel drive meant the Jeep could go almost anywhere. Its only fault was that it had a narrow wheelbase, which made it liable to roll over if it cornered too quickly.

After World War Two the American economy boomed. Production switched from tanks and planes to cars and fridges. Wages increased every year and this was reflected in the cars produced. Each year manufacturers brought out models that were bigger, flashier, and more curvaceous than before.

▼ 1948 Pontiac Silver Streak. In the U.S. after World War Two, cars were big and comfortable, with rounded, pre-war aerodynamic styling. But soon American cars were to echo new trends in aviation.

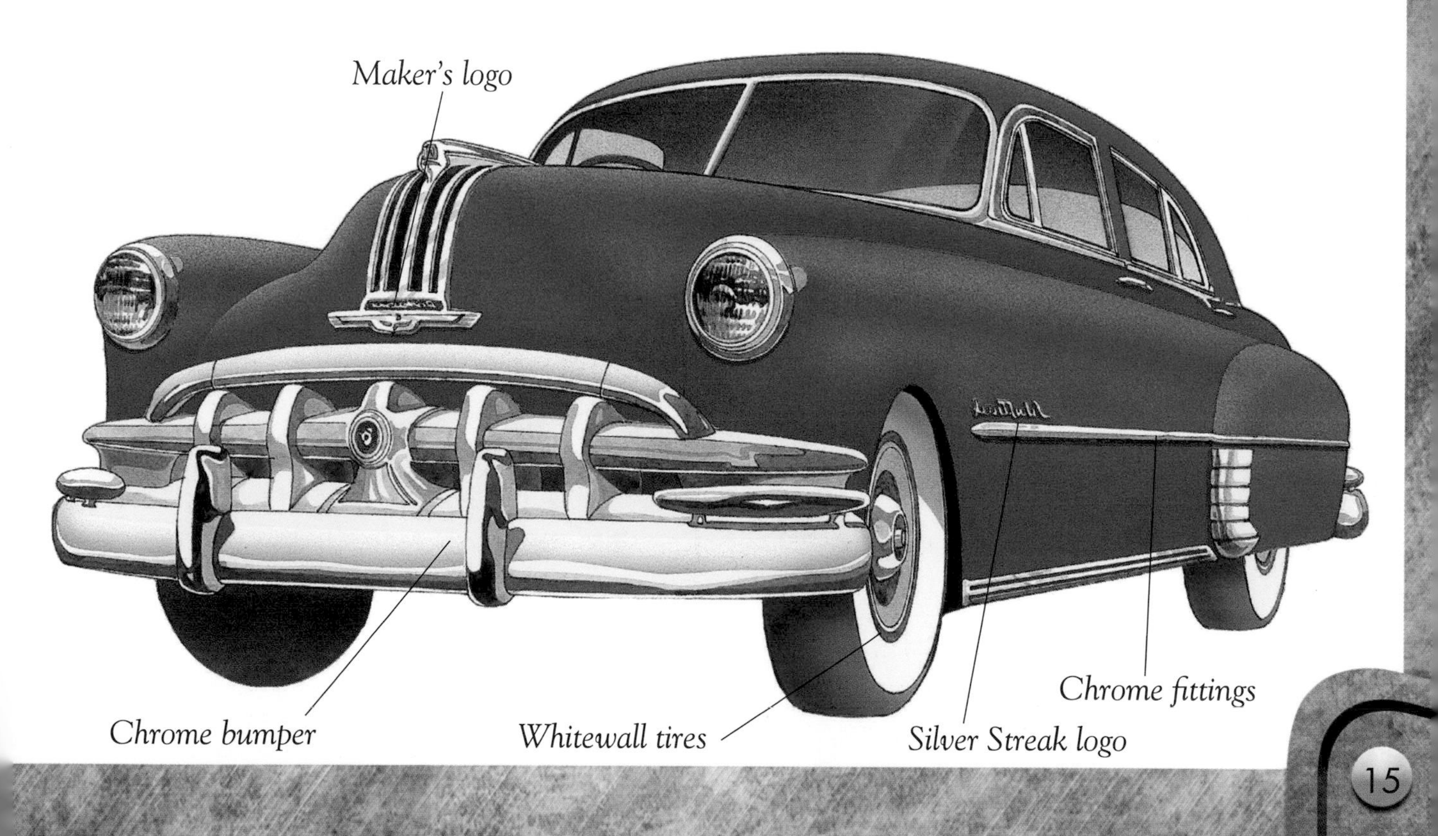

THE ROARING FIFTIES

▲ *The Volkswagen Beetle is a classic small car. Its name comes from its distinctive shape.*

Cars come in many shapes and sizes. American cars built in the 1950s and 1960s were large. Fuel was cheap, and the roads were wide and empty. Cadillacs, Fords, and Pontiacs were low, sleek, and very long. They had wraparound windshields, and some had metal "fins." Small European cars like the Mini Minor were designed to save money on gasoline. They could also squeeze into tiny parking spaces.

▲ *The Citroën Deux Chevaux, or 2CV, has a 2-horsepower engine. The name means "two horses."*

▼ The Morris Minor was one and a half times the size of a bubble car, but the Ford was as long as two bubble cars.

Metal "fin"

▼ The 1957 Pontiac was an American dream car. It was ideal for going to a drive-in movie or burger bar, with rock'n'roll playing on the radio.

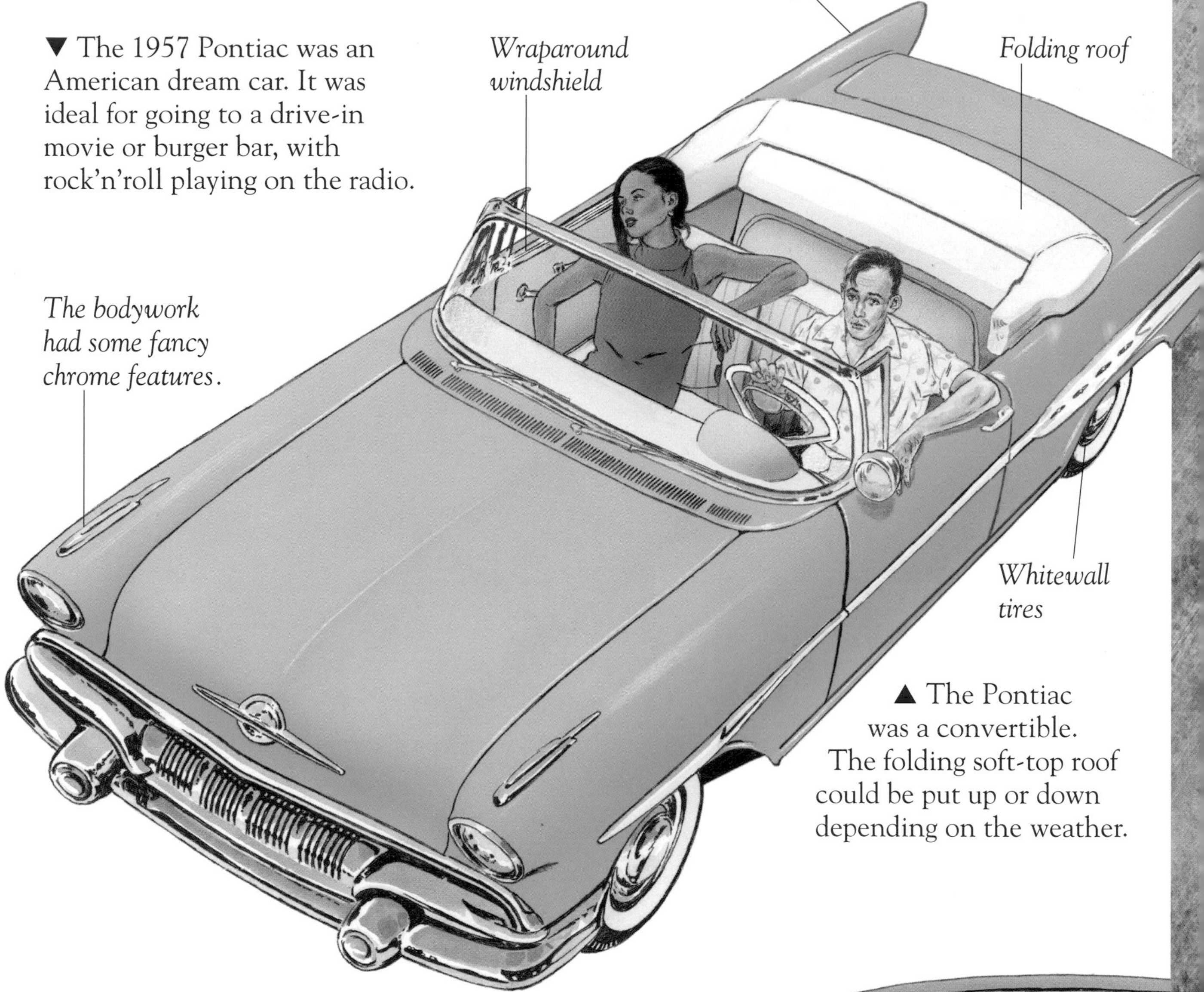

Wraparound windshield

Folding roof

The bodywork had some fancy chrome features.

Whitewall tires

▲ The Pontiac was a convertible. The folding soft-top roof could be put up or down depending on the weather.

▲ The Pontiac was nearly 19 feet long (6 m). Under the hood was a huge eight-cylinder engine. American dream cars were filled with features like power steering, reclining seats, and electric windows.

▶ Fins were introduced in 1955. They did not have a purpose, but customers liked the look of them.

SPORTS CARS

▲ *A 1935 Alfa Romeo with a supecharged 2.5-liter engine.*

Sports cars are road vehicles built for speed. Since the early 1950s, companies such as Porsche, Lotus, and Ferrari have made expensive, high-performance cars. These can reach speeds of at least 135 miles per hour (220 kph). Sports cars are low and sleek, and often have only two seats. They handle well and can tackle winding mountain roads at breakneck speeds.

The Italian company Alfa Romeo has made famous sports car since 1909.

Prince Henry Vauxhall, 1911.

▶ Early sports cars had open tops and wire-spoked tires. They had huge, powerful engines.

▼ The Porsche 911 first appeared in 1963. At the back it had a 2-liter high-performance engine. Its duck shape has been copied ever since.

Porsche 911

▶ Amphibious cars travel over land and water. In water, the wheels stop spinning and propellers take over.

Amphibious car, 1967

▼ Lotus has been winning races since 1948. The Esprit S4 can go from 0 to 60 miles per hour (100 kph) in 4.5 seconds and cruise at 160 miles per hour (260 kph).

The Esprit S4 cost more than ten times the cheapest tiny car. The Esprit has leather seats and air conditioning.

Lotus Esprit

Carrera

▶ This 1994 Porsche Carrera is a luxury version of the 911. It cost around $60,000.

HYBRID RACING CAR

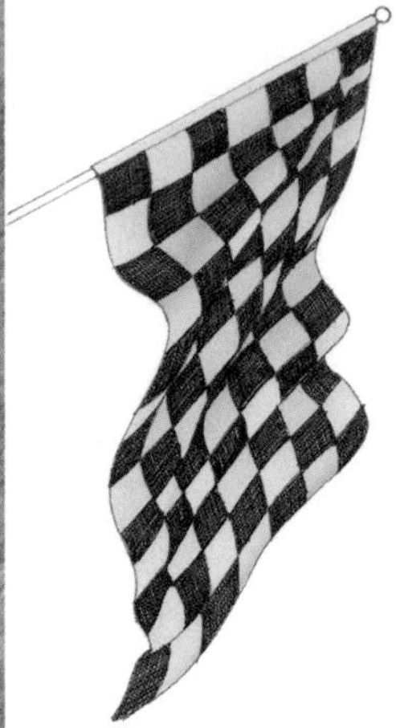

This hybrid racing car is designed for long-distance endurance races. It has two electric motors and a fuel efficient turbodiesel engine. It can switch to four-wheel drive at high speeds.

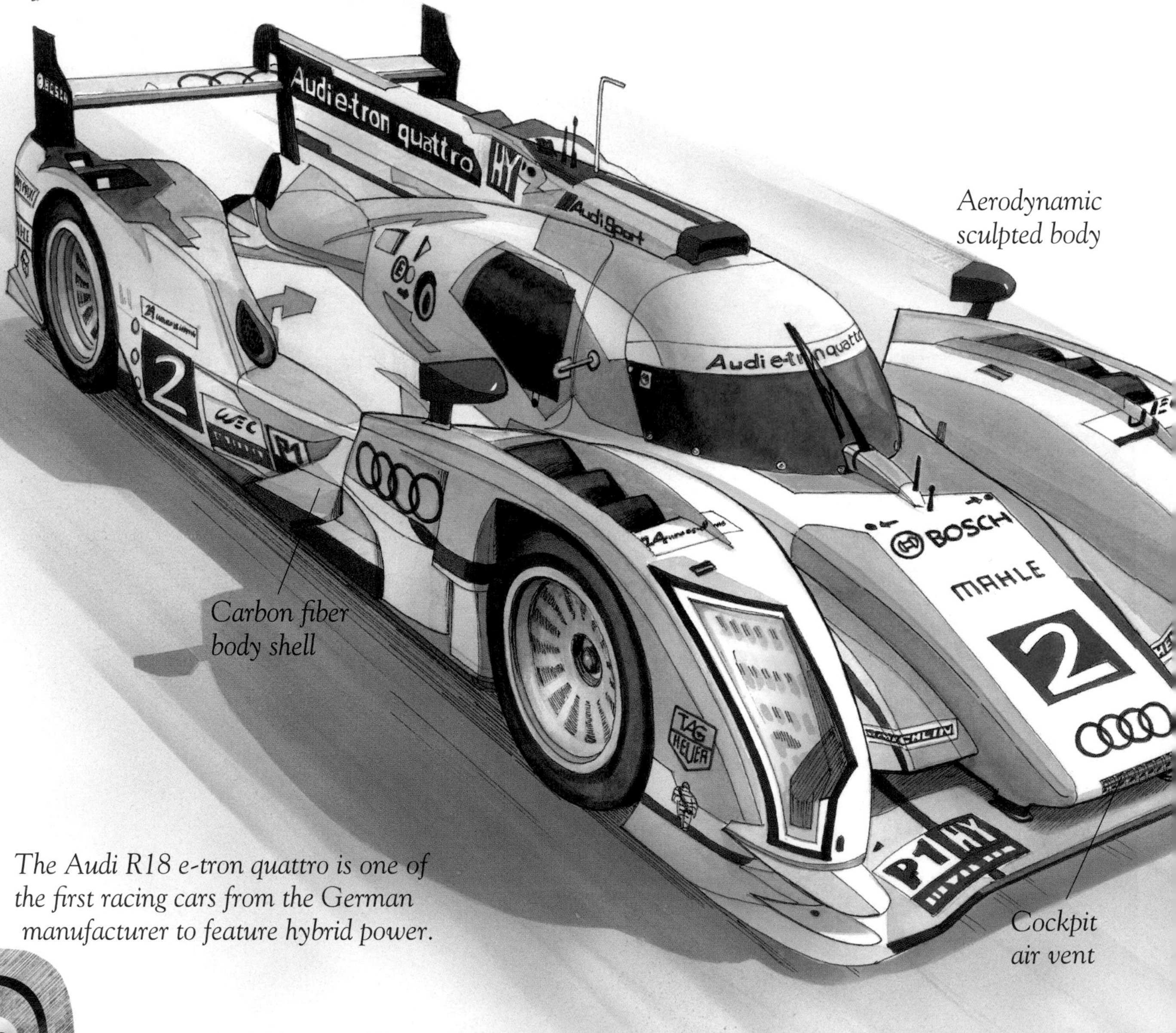

Audi e-tron quattro
Audi Sport
Audi e-tron quattro
BOSCH
MAHLE
2
2
TAG HEUER
P1 HY
Aerodynamic sculpted body
Carbon fiber body shell
Cockpit air vent

The Audi R18 e-tron quattro is one of the first racing cars from the German manufacturer to feature hybrid power.

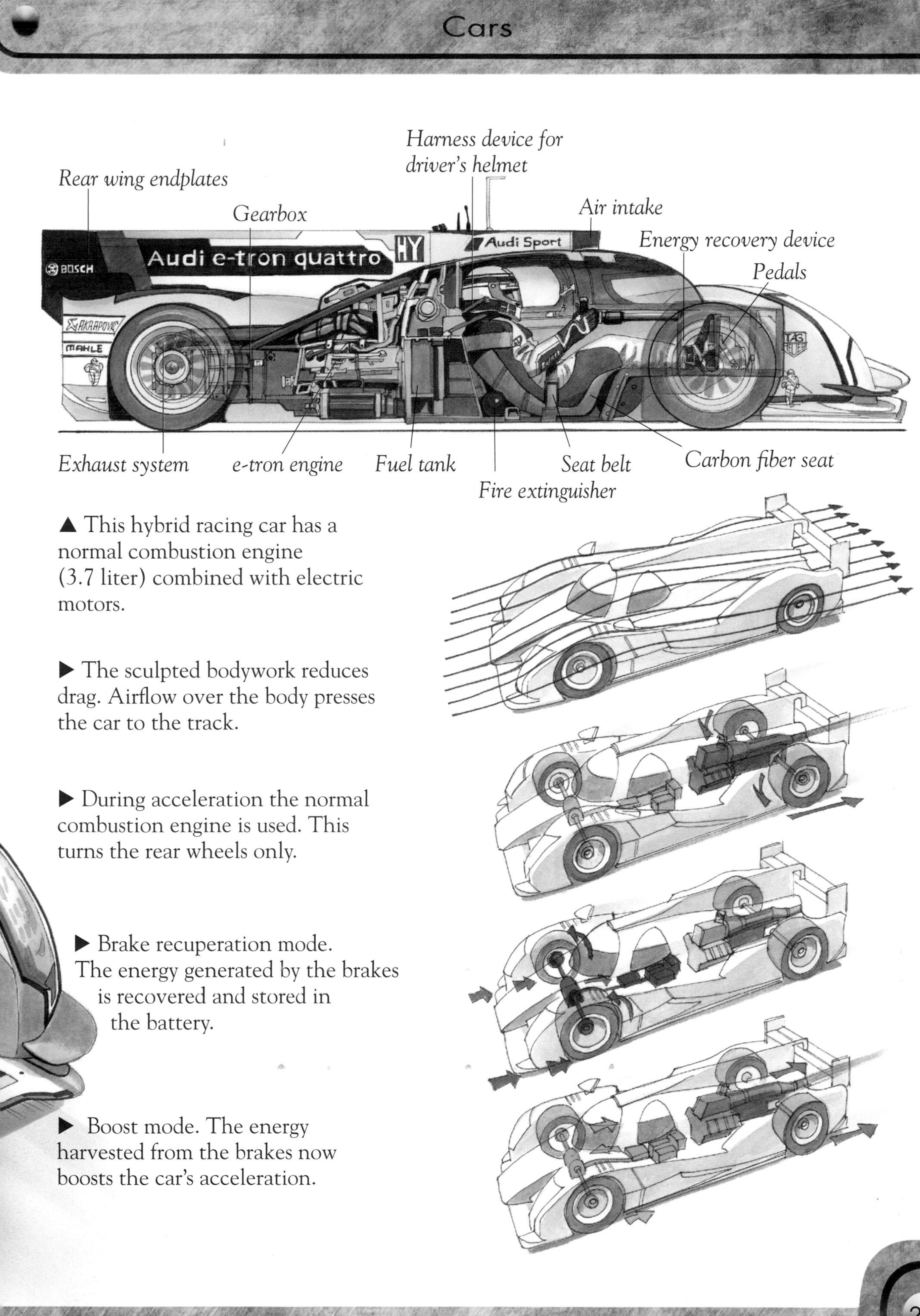

▲ This hybrid racing car has a normal combustion engine (3.7 liter) combined with electric motors.

▶ The sculpted bodywork reduces drag. Airflow over the body presses the car to the track.

▶ During acceleration the normal combustion engine is used. This turns the rear wheels only.

▶ Brake recuperation mode. The energy generated by the brakes is recovered and stored in the battery.

▶ Boost mode. The energy harvested from the brakes now boosts the car's acceleration.

HOW DO CARS WORK?

The engine is the driving force. It is usually at the front. A series of rods and shafts carries the force of the engine to the wheels. These spin around and drive the car forward. The steering wheel turns the front wheels and directs the car. Stepping on the brake pedal squeezes brake pads in the wheels, slowing them down. Shock absorbers above the wheel allow a smoother ride. Cool water is pumped through the radiator to prevent the engine from overheating. Waste gases from the engine leave by the exhaust pipe.

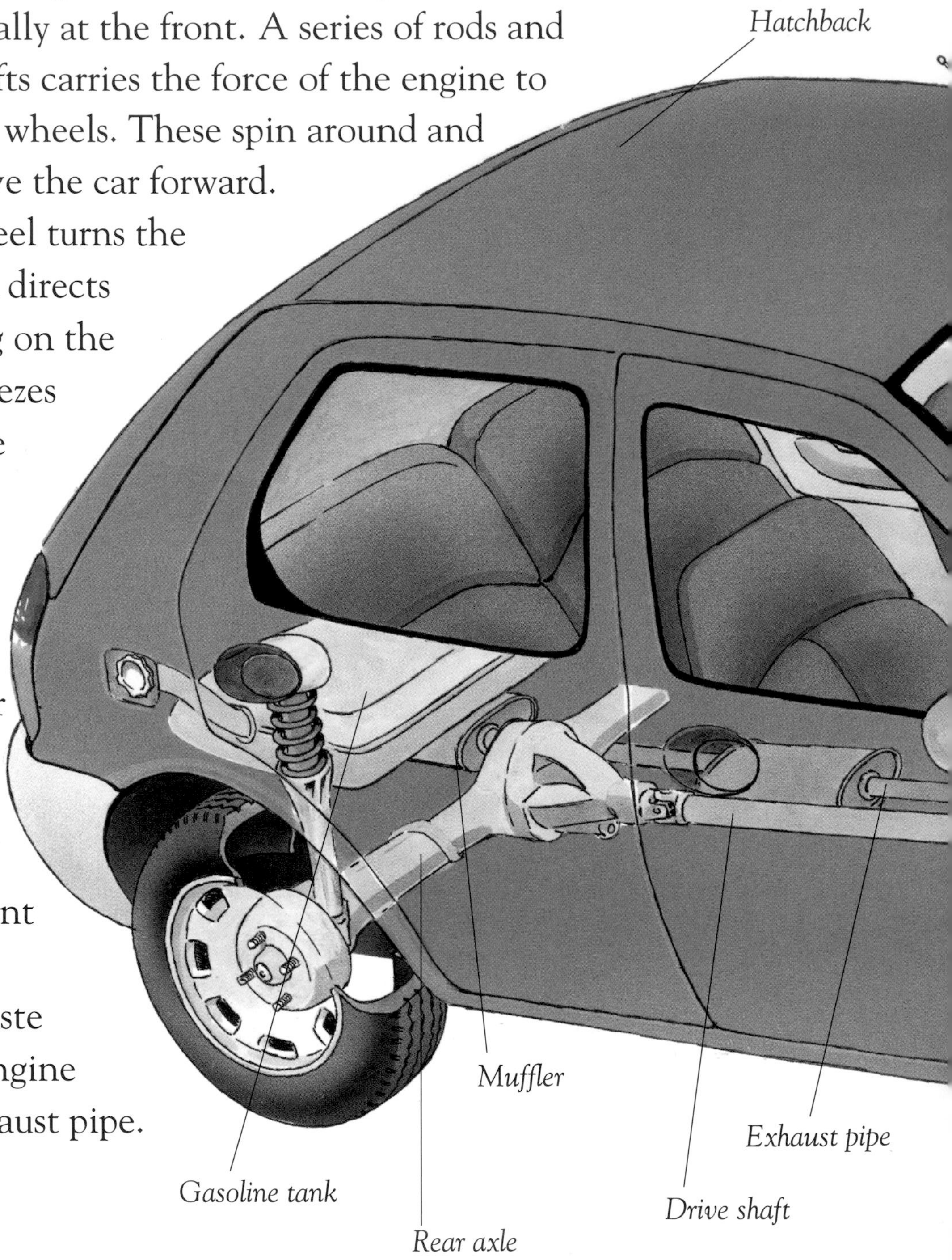

Hatchback

Muffler

Exhaust pipe

Gasoline tank

Drive shaft

Rear axle

Today's family car is small but powerful. The streamlined body makes the car fast and fuel-efficient. It can squeeze into small spaces, but inside it is surprisingly roomy.

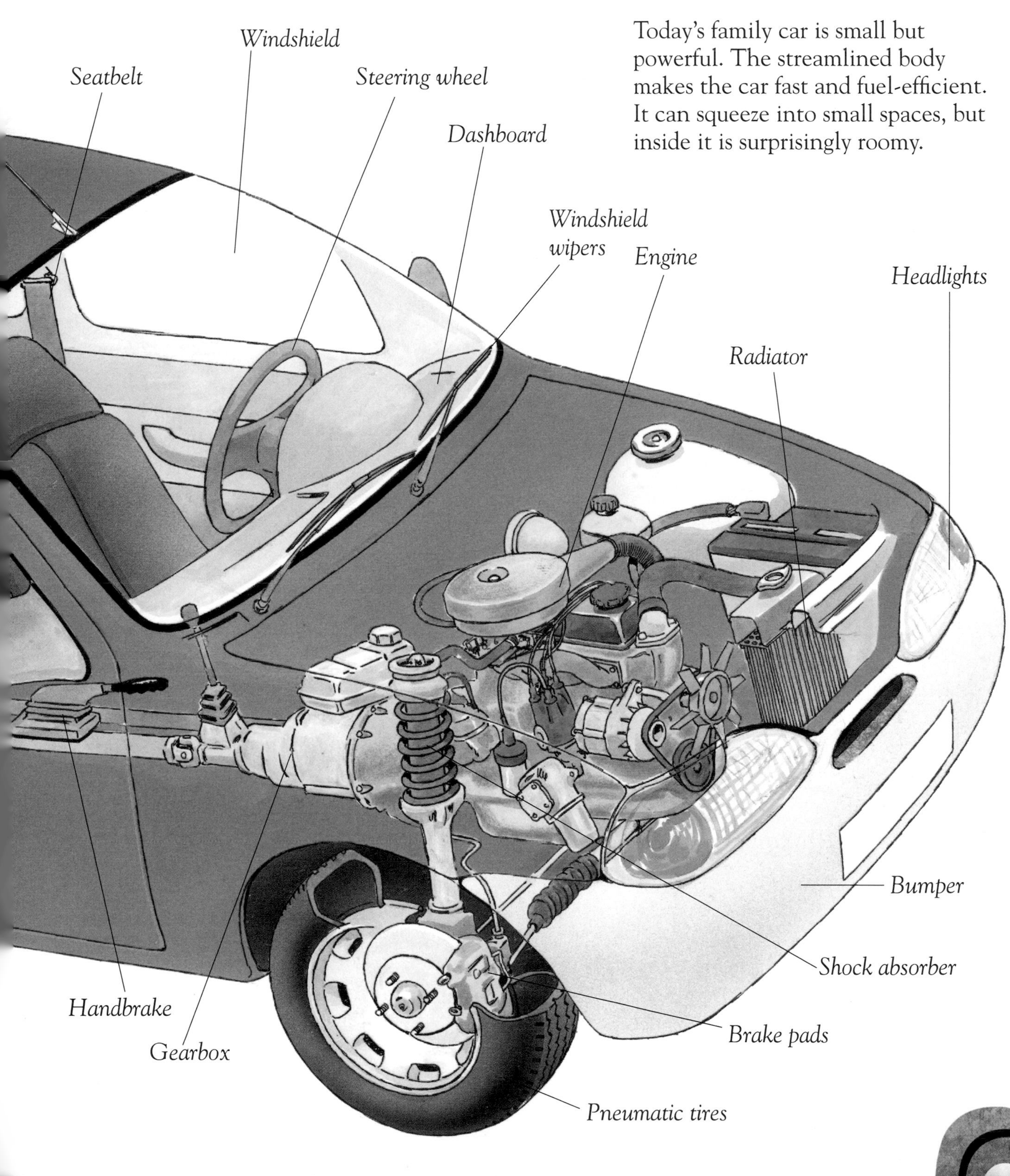

THE ENGINE

The engine is the driving force of a car. It works by a process known as internal combustion. This involves burning a fuel, usually gasoline, to release energy. The process takes place inside steel cylinders. Here a small amount of gasoline is mixed with air, and a spark ignites the mixture. The explosion moves a metal arm, called a piston. This pumps up and down with each explosion. A series of rods and gears carries this force to the wheels, which spin around and drive the car forward or backward.

▼ Four-stroke cycle in a cylinder.

Induction

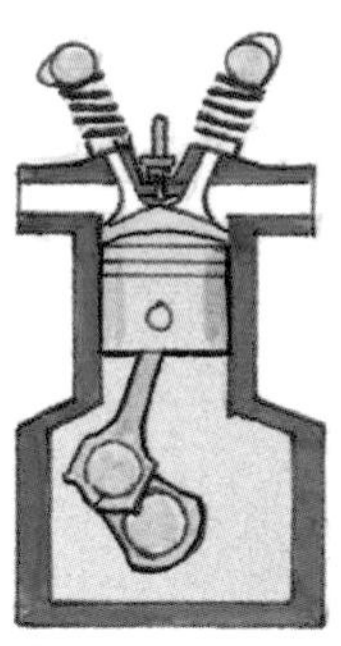

Compression

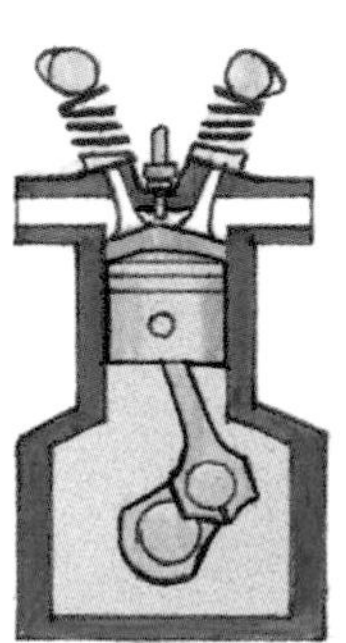

Ignition (the power stroke)

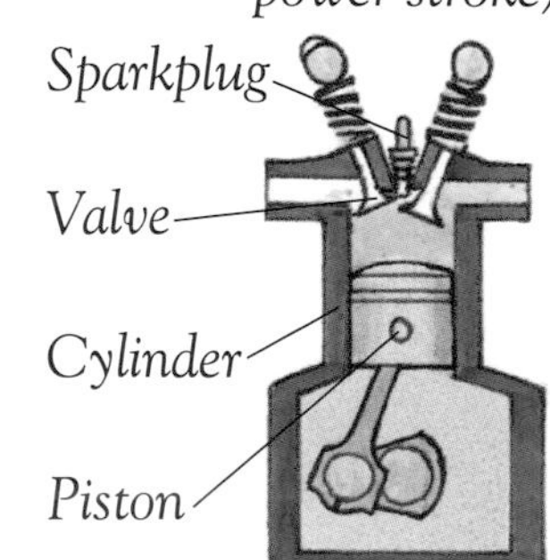

Exhaust

Clutch mechanism

The clutch is used to disconnect the engine from the rest of the transmission. With the clutch in, the driver can shift gears.

Cylinders fire one after the other to produce a spinning movement. Most cars have four cylinders, but powerful cars have six or eight.

The distributor is a rotating switch. It is connected to all the spark plugs, and it makes sure that they fire in the correct order.

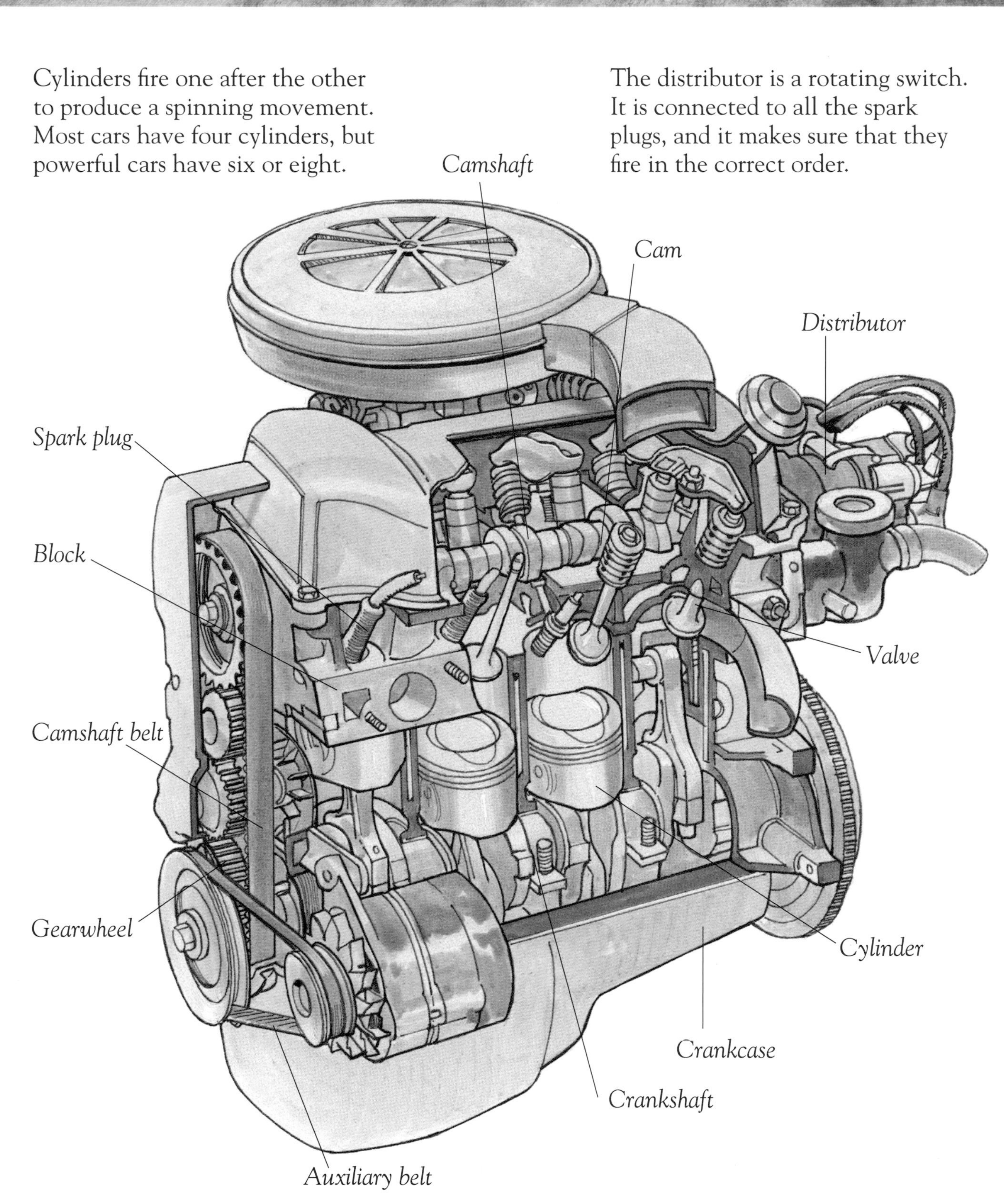

Oil keeps the engine running smoothly. Oil collects in the crankcase and is pushed back up into the block by a pump.

The crankshaft turns the up-and-down movement of the pistons into a circular movement to turn the wheels.

DEVELOPING A NEW CAR

Robot "arm"

▶ Robots can work nonstop, 24 hours a day. They can also perform many tasks that would be dangerous for human workers.

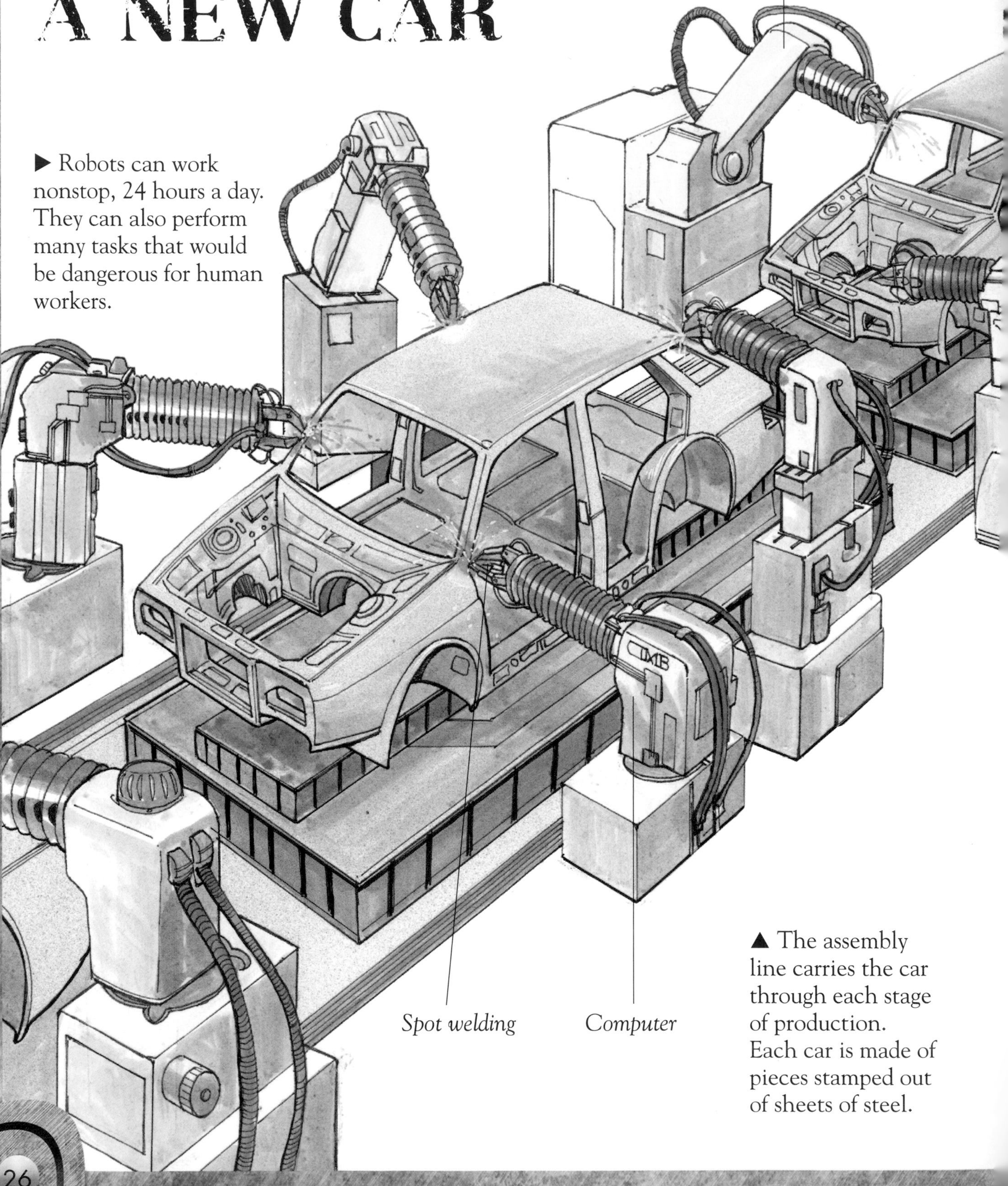

Spot welding

Computer

▲ The assembly line carries the car through each stage of production. Each car is made of pieces stamped out of sheets of steel.

◀ Robots can be programed to spot-weld, spray-paint, and drill engine parts. A small computer guides their "arms."

Developing a new car takes many years and costs millions of dollars. Car manufacturers have to be sure to get everything right, because any mistakes would be very costly. First, stylists and engineers listen to what drivers think of their present cars. They can then create new models using the latest technology and materials. Once the new design has been developed and tested thoroughly, mass production will start on the assembly line.

A CAD (computer-aided design) system helps the designer develop a new car. Computers can predict the effects of changes made as the design develops.

TODAY'S SPORTS CAR

The modern sports car is designed for both speed and sustainability. A plug-in hybrid with the appearance and breathtaking performance of a sports car, which at the same time exhibits the consumption and emissions of a compact car.

▼ The Toyota FT1 is a track-focused sports car model. The design draws on Toyota's sports car history.

▼ McLaren P1 is a limited production plug-in hybrid supercar. Shown for the first time at the 2013 Geneva Motor Show.

▶ The Ferrari LaFerrari sports car is styled like a ground-bound fighter jet. Its interior is custom-fit for its owner.

▼ The Lamborghini Huracán was released in 2014. It is equipped with four exhausts at the rear and an optional transparent engine cover.

▶ The BMW i8 is an new concept of sports car. Due to its intelligent light-weight construction and aerodynamic design, this model is far more efficient than most of its rivals.

USEFUL WORDS

Amphibious car A vehicle that is able to operate on land as well as on water.

Assembly line A step-by-step way of putting machinery together.

Beetle A nickname for the original Volkswagen car, launched in 1938.

Clutch Used for changing gears when the driver steps on the clutch pedal.

Cylinder The part of the car engine where combustion takes place.

Distributor A rotating switch that makes sure that spark plugs fire in the correct order.

Electric car A car that is powered by an electric battery and not fuel like most cars.

Horseless carriages Engine-powered cars from the late 1800s that looked like horse-drawn carriages.

Pneumatic tire A hollow tire, usually made of rubber, that is filled with air.

Radiator A device which circulates water to cool a car engine.

Shock absorbers A car's suspension system which helps to smooth out the ride.

Solar power Using energy from the sun's rays to provide power.

Tin Lizzy A nickname for the Model T Ford.

Welding Joining pieces of metal using heat.

TIMELINE

1769 A three-wheeled steam-powered tractor is built by Frenchman Nicolas-Joseph Cugnot.

1898 The British electric car *l'Elephant* is one of six electric entries in the 1898 Auto Club de France race.

1903 The Ford Motor Company is founded in Detroit, Michigan.

1909 The "Spirit of Ecstasy" ornament is added to the Rolls-Royce hood.

1932 The first Bugatti Royale Type 41 is sold.

1940 The U.S. army four-wheel-drive Jeep becomes world famous.

1948 The Morris Minor car appears, it was designed by Alec Issigonis.

1958 The Mini (again, by Issigonis) is the first car to have a combined front engine and gearbox across the chassis.

1963 The Porsche 911 first appeared with a two-liter high-performance engine.

1975 Italian Lella Lombardi becomes the first woman to drive in a season of Formula 1 Grand Prix races.

1990 Production of the Beetle reaches 21 million, more than any other car.

2013 The McLaren P1 hybrid car is shown for the first time in Geneva.

2014 The Lamborghini Huracán is released. It was designed by Lamborghini's design chief Filippo Perini.

INDEX